AIR SHOW JETS

MotoR Mania

by Matt Doeden

Richard Bihler, consultant and pilot

Technical Sergeant Justin D. Pyle, photojournalist, U.S. Air Force Demonstration Squadron

Lerner Publications Company • Minneapolis

For Mom

Cover Photo: Two U.S. Air Force Thunderbirds perform a stunt in 2007.

Lerner Publications Company
A division of Lerner Publishing Group, Inc.
241 First Avenue North
Minneapolis, MN 55401 U.S.A.

Website address: www.lernerbooks.com

Library of Congress Cataloging-in-Publication Data

Doeden, Matt.
    Air show jets / by Matt Doeden.
      p.   cm. — (Motor mania)
    Includes bibliographical references and index.
    ISBN 978–0–8225–9430–7 (lib. bdg. : alk. paper)
    1. Air shows—Juvenile literature. 2. Jet planes,
Military—Juvenile literature. 3. Stunt flying—
Juvenile literature. I. Title.
    TL506.A1D64 2009
    797.5'4—dc22   2008025572

Manufactured in the United States of America
1 2 3 4 5 6 – DP – 14 13 12 11 10 09

Contents

Four bright blue jets streak across the sky at almost 400 miles (644 kilometers) per hour. Thin lines of colored smoke follow behind the planes, painting the sky. The deep, loud rumble of the planes' powerful jet engines fills the air and shakes the ground. The planes fly in a tight diamond formation, with their wingtips less than 2 feet (0.6 meters) apart. Even the tiniest mistake could spell disaster for all four pilots.

This is precision flying at its highest level. It's the result of hundreds of hours of hard work and practice by the pilots who fly the jets and the crews that keep the planes in top condition.

People flock to air shows around the world. They love to see old planes on display, meet pilots, and learn more about flight. But the flight demonstration (demo) teams flying jets are always the biggest attractions. Teams like the U.S. Navy's Blue Angels, the U.S. Air Force's Thunderbirds, the Canadian Snowbirds, and Britain's Royal Air Force (RAF) Red Arrows thrill and amaze audiences. Their breathtaking aerial displays show what these amazing airplanes can do.

Four Blue Angels fly a diamond formation at an air show in 2007.

Chapter One

AIR SHOW JET HISTORY

This airplane won the long-distance prize at the first air show in 1909.

Almost since the airplane was invented in 1903, pilots have been pushing the limits of flight. The first air show took place in 1909. Airplane races were often the main attraction in these shows. Three years later, a U.S. Navy demo team was simulating air battles, or dogfights, for excited audiences.

The appeal of the airplane and the air show grew from there. In World War I (1914–1918), airplanes proved to be useful in battle. The militaries of the United States, Britain, Germany, and other countries spent a lot of time and money developing airplanes for battle. The planes got bigger, faster, and more reliable. And the militaries loved to show off what their planes and pilots

could do in the air. Early flight demo teams like the U.S. Navy's Sea Hawks thrilled air show crowds with spins, loops, and other daring tricks.

Military pilots weren't the only ones showing off their skills, though. By the 1920s, barnstorming had become a popular form of entertainment. Barnstormers were stunt pilots who traveled around the world. Many of the pilots were former World War I pilots who wanted to make a living by flying. They put on a sort of flying circus, with aerial stunts from loops to the dangerous wing walking. Most barnstormers traveled in large groups, but some performed alone. Most of them flew simple biplanes—planes with two sets of wings stacked one on top of the other.

Barnstormers Gladys Roy *(left)* and Ivan Unger play tennis at 3,000 feet (915 m) as part of a 1925 wing walking stunt.

The Blue Angels Emerge

Airplanes were an important weapon in World War II (1939–1945). The technology had come a long way since World War I. Fighter planes like the P-51 Mustang made flight seem more glamorous than ever. But when the war ended, the U.S. military had lots of planes and pilots but not much for them to do. It was time for flight demo teams to take a big step forward.

The navy knew that airplanes and pilots fascinated the public. So in 1946, navy officials formed a new flight demo team. The team's mission was to help with naval recruiting and promote the image of the navy. At first, the team was called simply the Navy Flight Exhibition Team.

The navy put experienced pilot Roy "Butch" Voris in charge of building and leading the new team. Voris picked the Grumman F6F Hellcat as

Four U.S. Army P-51 Mustangs fly in formation over Italy during World War II.

What's in a Name?

Navy officials knew that they needed a flashier name for the Flight Exhibition Team. They narrowed down the choices to two—the Blue Angels and the Blue Lancers. But they couldn't decide which one to use. Luckily, the press made the decision for them. The debate between the names leaked, and the press started calling the team the Blue Angels. The name stuck.

Left: The Blue Angels take off in their F6F Hellcats for their first public air show on June 15, 1946.
Below: Roy "Butch" Voris was the first commander of the Blue Angels.

the team's plane. The Hellcat had been one of the most successful U.S. fighter planes in World War II. This propeller-driven fighter could reach speeds of 380 miles (610 km) per hour. More important, it was responsive and easy to handle. The Hellcat seemed like the perfect plane to show off the navy's aerial ability.

The Blue Angels ground crew modified the planes for show. They made the planes lighter by removing guns and other combat parts. They painted the planes bright blue and gold—colors that would become the team's trademark. Voris, his team of young pilots, and their planes started training in the spring of 1946. They made their first demo flight on June 15. Their simple aerial demo was an instant hit.

Enter the Jets

The Blue Angels went through a lot of changes in the early years. In August 1946, they switched to the Grumman F8F Bearcat, a smaller, faster version of the Hellcat. But it was only a temporary change. Jet engine technology had taken off in the mid-1940s. Jet engines work by pulling in cool air and heating it, forcing it out of the back of the engine to provide thrust. Jets were much faster and more powerful than propeller-driven aircraft.

The Thunderbirds fly in F–100 Super Sabres in 1956.

So in August 1949, the Blue Angels switched to jets—the F9F-2 Panther. The powerful Panther blew away the old propeller-driven planes, reaching speeds of 575 miles (925 km) per hour. The era of the air show jet had begun.

The Blue Angels weren't alone, though. The U.S. Air Force had formed after the war. It started a demo team of its own in 1953. The team would eventually take the name Thunderbirds. For the first two years, the new team flew the F-84G Thunderjet. This powerful fighter-bomber had seen heavy action in the Korean War (1950–1953). In 1955 the team switched to the F-84F Thunderstreak. Finally, a year later, they settled on the F-100 Super Sabre.

Jet Turbine Engine

Jet engines create power, or thrust, by rapidly heating air. Air comes into the engine through the intake. A fan and a compressor push the air into a combustion chamber. This chamber is where the jet's fuel is burned. The air heats up very quickly inside this chamber.

As air heats, it expands. This results in greater air pressure inside the chamber. The pressure forces the air across the turbines. The hot, pressurized air spins the turbines at a high speed. The energy pushed out by the turbines is what gives the jet its thrust.

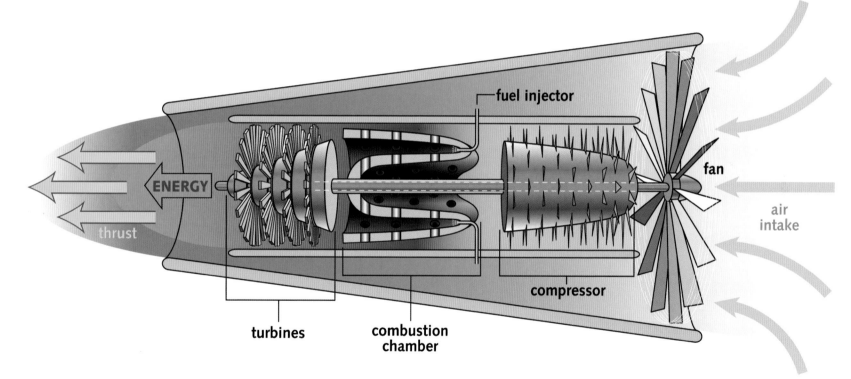

The team thrived while flying the F-100. The Super Sabre's powerful turbojet engine made it the air force's first supersonic fighter. That means it could go faster than the speed of sound—about 770 miles (1,238 km) per hour. The F-100's speed and precise handling made it the new standard among air show jets. The Thunderbirds would go on to fly it for the next 13 years. The Blue Angels joined the Thunderbirds in flying supersonic jets in 1957, when they switched to the F11F-1 Tiger.

Disaster with the F-105B

The Thunderbirds briefly switched to the F-105B Thunderchief in 1964. But during one of the team's steep climbs, the plane of Captain Gene Devlin suffered a failure, resulting in Devlin's death. The team quickly switched back to the trusty F-100 Super Sabre. They flew a total of only six shows in the F-105B.

A Worldwide Passion

The United States wasn't the only nation that wanted its own demo teams. Britain's Royal Air Force had formed its own demo teams for decades. The teams had names like the Black Arrows, the Red Pelicans, and the Yellowjackets. In 1964 the RAF decided that it needed just one team. So it formed the Red Arrows.

The team took to the air in their Folland Gnat trainer planes. The Gnat was small and not very fast, but it was easy to fly. It could fly in tight formations, do rolls, and make high-speed passes—all the moves that made for a great precision demo. In 1968 the Red Arrows started flying the formation that they're best known for—the Diamond Nine. This formation features nine planes flying in a diamond pattern.

The Canadian Forces formed a full-time team of its own in 1971. The 431 Air Demonstration Squadron, better known as the Snowbirds, flew

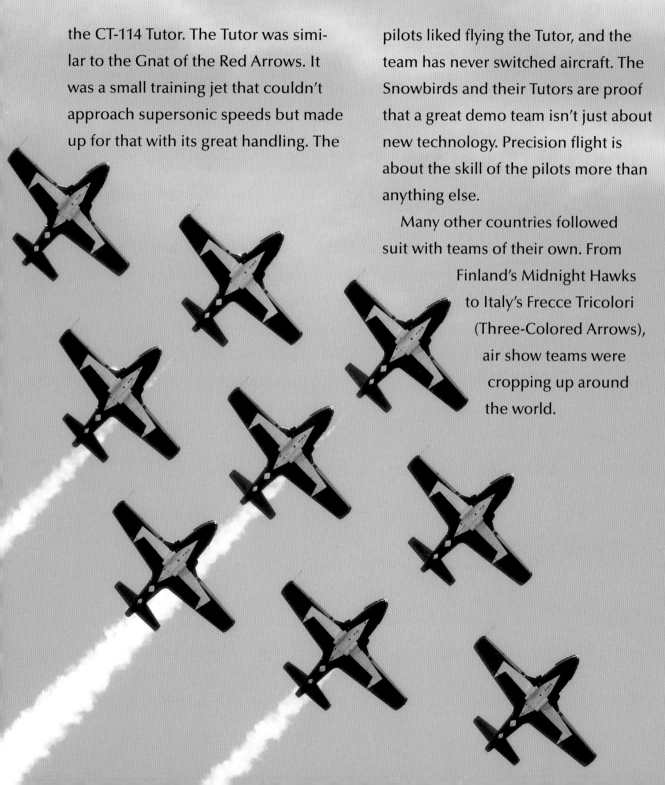

the CT-114 Tutor. The Tutor was similar to the Gnat of the Red Arrows. It was a small training jet that couldn't approach supersonic speeds but made up for that with its great handling. The pilots liked flying the Tutor, and the team has never switched aircraft. The Snowbirds and their Tutors are proof that a great demo team isn't just about new technology. Precision flight is about the skill of the pilots more than anything else.

Many other countries followed suit with teams of their own. From Finland's Midnight Hawks to Italy's Frecce Tricolori (Three-Colored Arrows), air show teams were cropping up around the world.

The Canadian Snowbirds perform a diamond nine during an air show in Quebec, Canada.

Changes in the Air

Change was a near constant for the big demo teams over the next several decades. By the early 1970s, both the Thunderbirds and the Blue Angels were flying the F-4 Phantom II. The F-4 was unlike any plane either team had flown before. It was bigger, heavier, and a lot more powerful. But for precision flying—where tight handling is a lot more important than raw power—that wasn't really a good thing. The planes were involved in several accidents, some of which resulted in deaths. They were also expensive to maintain and fuel.

For these reasons, the F-4 didn't last long with either team. The

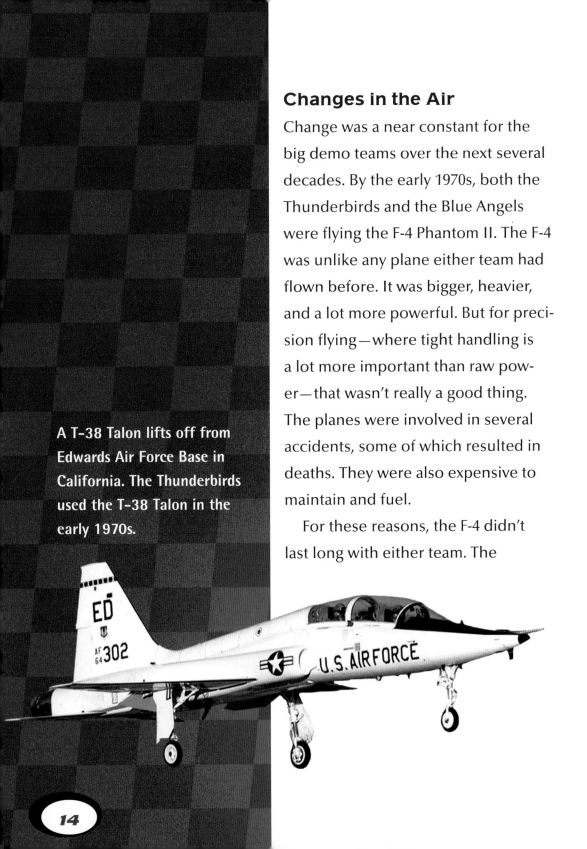

A T–38 Talon lifts off from Edwards Air Force Base in California. The Thunderbirds used the T–38 Talon in the early 1970s.

Thunderbirds switched to the T-38 Talon, a sleek, maneuverable trainer jet, in 1974. Later that year, the Blue Angels abandoned the F-4 as well. They switched to the A-4F Skyhawk, a fighter that had seen heavy action in the Vietnam War (1957–1975). For both teams, the new planes were cheaper and, because they handled so well, they provided a better show. And most important, they were safer.

Change was in the air for the Red Arrows as well. After almost two decades in the Gnat, the team switched to the BAE Hawk trainer jet. The Hawk, like the Gnat, is a subsonic plane—it can't fly faster than sound. But it's ideal for formation flying (multiple planes flying together in a pattern). It perfectly suited the purposes of the Red Arrows, which had never focused on speed.

Into the Twenty-First Century

As the 1980s rolled around, jet technology wasn't standing still, so teams did their best to keep up. The Thunderbirds switched to the F-16A Fighting Falcon in 1983. The Fighting Falcon was a fully modern fighting machine. Entering service in 1978, it was designed to be the workhorse of the U.S. Air Force fleet. Its combination of speed—it can reach speeds of 1,345 miles (2,165 km) per hour—and handling made it perfect for the Thunderbirds. The team switched to a later version of the Fighting Falcon, the F-16C, in 1992.

The Blue Angels, meanwhile, were also ready for a newer, more modern jet. After the 1986 season, the team

Two F-16 Thunderbirds do a opposing knife edge pass.

U.S. Air Force major Nicole Malachowski *(second from right)* prepares to climb into her F16-C Fighting Falcon. She was the first female pilot on the U.S. Air Force Thunderbirds.

switched to the F/A-18 Hornet. The Hornet had entered navy service in 1983 and was a capable and deadly fighter. Its two powerful engines push it to speeds of more than 1,200 miles (1,932 km) per hour. But the plane handles well at slower speeds, which appealed to the Blue Angels squad.

The teams kept performing throughout the 1990s and 2000s. In 2005 the Thunderbirds made news by selecting Nicole Malachowski as a pilot. She became the first female pilot the team had ever had. Her first performance with the team came in March 2006.

In April 2007, the Blue Angels were in the news for a much sadder reason—tragedy. The team was performing its demo in South Carolina. In the final minutes of the demo, just before landing, pilot Kevin Davis lost control of his plane. The audience saw a fireball and a cloud of black smoke. His Super Hornet crashed into the ground, killing Davis. The accident was a grim reminder that precision flying is a dangerous job. But pilots accept the risk. Most of them believe it's worth it to be a part of one of the greatest demo teams in the world.

This illustration shows all the aircraft used by the Blue Angels from 1946 *(top)* to 2004.

Chapter Two

AIR SHOW JET CULTURE

*T*here's no better place to see airplanes—new and old—than at an air show. Air shows held around the world vary in size. Some feature just a few aircraft. Others are major productions with thousands of planes and dozens of demonstrations. Some of the shows draw hundreds of thousands of people. For many shows, the atmosphere is almost like a carnival, with souvenir shops, concession stands, and much more.

Shows can take place in all sorts of locations. People may crowd onto open fields. Or they may gather along a lake or ocean shore while the planes fly over the water. The Chicago Air & Water Show is one of the most popular shows. Fans line the streets of Chicago along the shores of Lake

Michigan. Crowds stretch for miles watching one display after the next.

Many air shows feature vintage aircraft, such as World War II fighters, as well as some of the latest technology. Military helicopters, cargo planes, bombers, training planes, and other jets may round out the show. The planes are cleaned, waxed, and ready to impress their audience.

Military demo teams aren't the only draw. Private teams fly their own airplanes in the spirit of the old barnstormers. Some fly old propeller-driven planes, while others fly jets. The L-39 Patriots, for example, fly the

More than one million people gathered in Chicago for the 45th annual Chicago Air & Water Show in 2003.

Spectators at an air show in Jacksonville, Florida, look at military aircraft in 2006.

L-39C Albatross, a trainer jet. They perform a lot of the aerials that the military teams do. Private teams get most of their money from sponsorships. Companies pay them for ads on their uniforms and planes, much like a car racing team.

Solo military jets can also put on shows. These single jets fly tactical demos. The demos are designed to show off a plane's combat abilities. For example, a tactical demo may include a short, loud takeoff; a steep climb; blazing fast speeds; and very sharp turns. The pilot may also do multiple rolls and simulate weapons fire, complete with preplanned fireworks on the ground.

But the highlight of any show is an appearance by the Blue Angels, Thunderbirds, or other military demo team. From the moment the team arrives, the excitement grows and grows. The crowd gathers as the pilots climb into their planes and take off. The fans watch each move and stunt, gasping and cheering. It's as thrilling for the fans as it is for the pilots themselves.

An F/A-18 Hornet takes off.

A Dangerous Pursuit

Danger has always been a part of air show flying. Pilots push their skills and their planes to the limit. Small pilot errors or problems with the plane can lead to disaster. Accidents are rare, but they do happen. One of the worst accidents happened on January 18, 1982. The Thunderbirds were practicing a move called the four-plane diamond loop. In this move, the lead plane controls the movement. The other planes follow the leader. But a problem with the lead plane's control stick caused the plane to crash into the ground. The other three planes followed behind. All four pilots in the crash were killed.

Making a Team

Flying on a military demo team takes skill, concentration, and lots of practice. Spots on teams like the Blue Angels and the Thunderbirds are hard to get. The competition is fierce. Pilots must be experienced.

The members of the 2007 U.S. Navy Blue Angels meet with U.S. president George W. Bush on the lawn of the White House.

Every team has its own requirements of flight hours needed. For example, a Thunderbirds pilot must have flown at least 750 hours in a tactical jet such as the Hornet, the Super Hornet, or the F-14 Tomcat.

The selection process is long and tough. It varies from team to team, but the basics are the same. Team officials review each pilot's flight history. The pilots go through a series of hard physical and mental tests. Team officials also watch their ability to get along with the rest of the team. Demo pilots spend a lot of time together. They must trust one another completely. So fitting in is a big part of being chosen for a team.

Finally, the choices are made. The "newbies" have a lot to learn. They study the demo and learn it by heart. Before they ever practice it in the air, they learn to visualize the entire routine. Then it's finally time to practice. The team takes it easy at first. They let the newbies get the feel for the planes and the demo. They give one another plenty of room between planes. There's no need to take any chances.

The work isn't over when the planes land, though. Then it's time for pilots to grade themselves and one another on the flight. They talk about any mistakes they made. They watch the practice on video. They look for any small error and then work to fix it. Over weeks of practice, their formations get tighter and tighter. The moves get faster and more precise. Soon the team is ready to begin its season.

Working Your Way Down

A finely tuned demo happens as close to the ground as is safely possible, so it's more impressive to fans. But flying low is dangerous. Early on in their training, teams practice at high altitudes. That gives them more margin for error. As they get better and the demo is perfected, they move down to lower and lower altitudes.

Even trained pilots have to learn a lot before becoming demo team pilots. A potential Thunderbird pilot is flying in this F-16 Fighting Falcon.

Team Positions

Pilots are the most visible part of any demo team. They're the ones that people come to see. Most teams number their planes and their pilots. In the Blue Angels, the commander, or boss, flies plane number 1. The others in the main group are numbers 2, 3, and 4. The Blue Angels also have two solo pilots. They are numbers 5 and 6.

The numbering system is different for each team. The Snowbirds have nine planes. But the idea is the same. A pilot always flies in the same position for every demo. That builds the consistency and confidence that are so important for this type of flying.

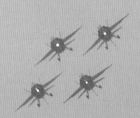

Four Blue Angels fly by the Golden Gate Bridge in San Francisco, California, during a practice run for an air show.

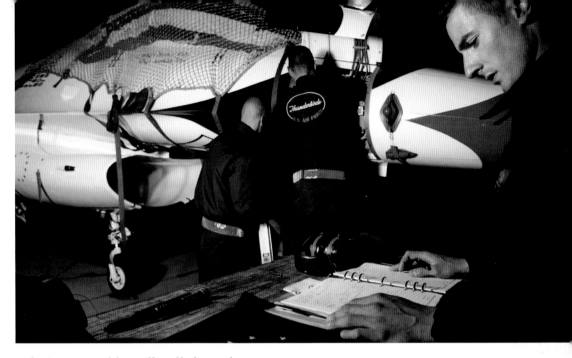

The pilots are only part of the team, though. Some teams have their own narrator. The narrator talks to the audience during the demo. This team member explains the formations and moves as they happen overhead. The flight surgeon is in charge of the health of the pilots and other crew members. The ground crew helps the team prepare for flight. Crew chiefs are in charge of keeping the planes in shape and getting them ready for a show. Other team members help set up schedules, work on public relations, and handle all the other problems that come up. Without this group of people, the pilots could never do their jobs.

Pilots aren't the only teammembers. *Top:* Staff Sergeant Patrick Mahoney looks over paperwork, while mechanics do late night maintenance. *Bottom:* These navy mechanics are doing winter maintenance to keep the F/A-18A Hornets in top condition.

Fat Albert

The Blue Angels use a huge C-130 Hercules plane called Fat Albert to move from show to show. Fat Albert carries all the ground crew and other team members, as well as their gear. The C-130 can carry up to 42,000 pounds (19,051 kilograms). This is about the same weight as 12 midsize cars! The Blue Angels' C-130 even makes a brief appearance during the demo.

The Demo

The demo is what it's all about for both the fans and the pilots. The maneuvers are different for each team. But the basics are the same. The demo is a combination of tight formation flying, coordinated rolls, loops, high-speed passes, and other exciting stunts. For the fans on the ground, it's a chance to sit back and soak in the sights, sounds, and smells of these highly tuned jets. Fans of all ages bring their binoculars, cameras, and often earplugs to enjoy the show.

Formation flying is at the center of any demo. The four-plane diamond formation may be the most famous. The lead plane takes the spot in front of the diamond. Two wingmen fall in behind on each side of the leader. The slot pilot completes the diamond, flying behind the wingmen. Other popular formations include the echelon (a diagonal line), the delta (a six-plane triangle), and the line abreast (planes flying side by side).

Left: The Thunderbirds perform an echelon formation during an air show in 2003. *Above:* Blue Angels perform a diamond roll.

This picture was taken from the cockpit of a Blue Angels F/A-18 Hornet while the team was performing a diamond roll. Pilots use a wing tip, a mark, or a letter to spot where they should be.

Formation flying requires intense concentration. Planes may be only a couple of feet apart. Even a small mistake can spell disaster. Pilots often use a technique called spot flying. Only the leader looks ahead. The other pilots focus on a single spot on a plane next to them. The spot could be a small mark, a wingtip, or a letter on the side of the plane. They hold their position by keeping that spot in the same place in their view. It's hard work. But to the audience, it looks almost effortless.

This photograph, taken in 2007, shows what the pilot sees while executing a diamond roll. Lieutenant Colonel Kevin Robbins looks past his back seat passenger to spot on the plane next to his.

Formations

Here are a few popular air show formations.

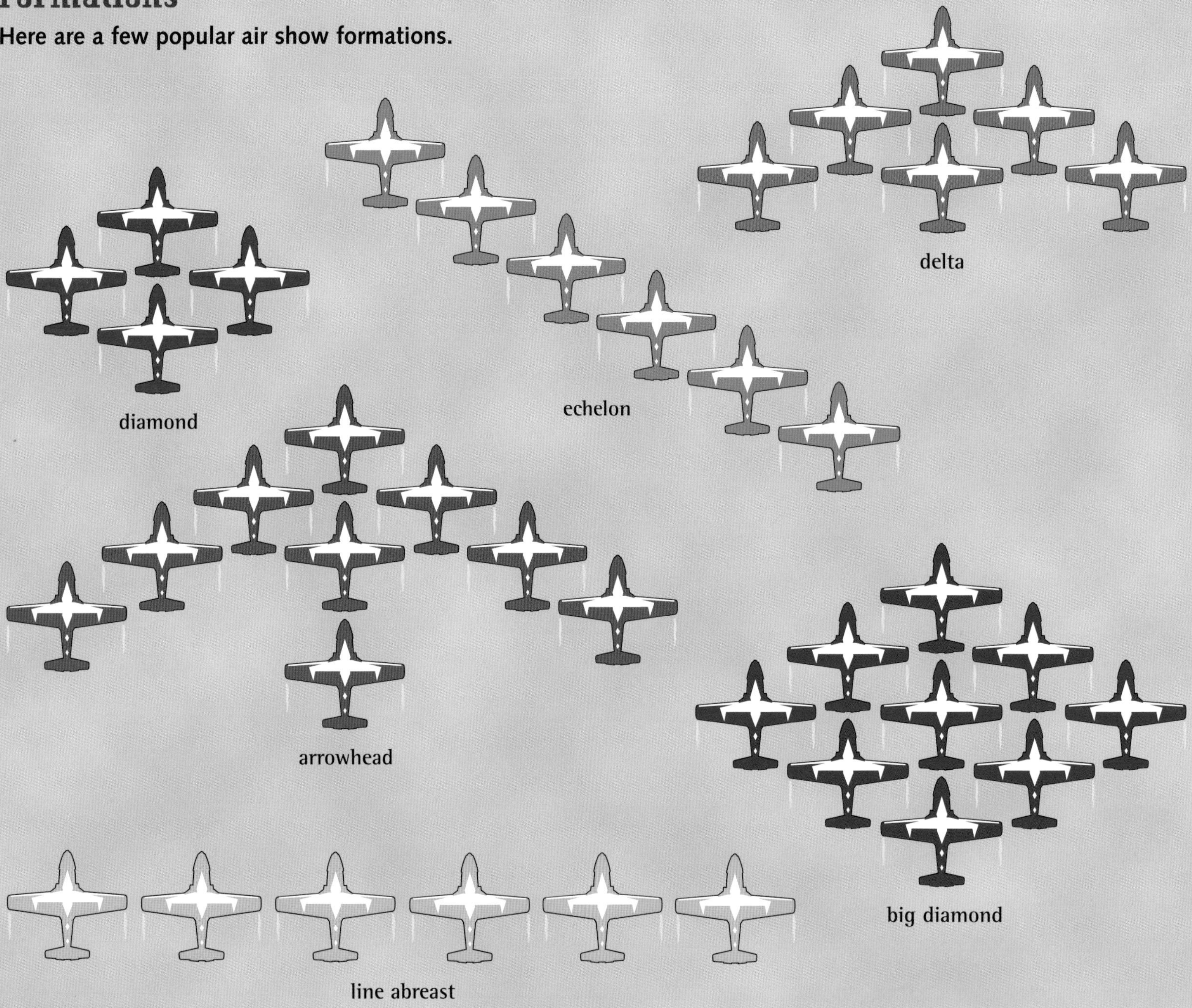

diamond

echelon

delta

arrowhead

big diamond

line abreast

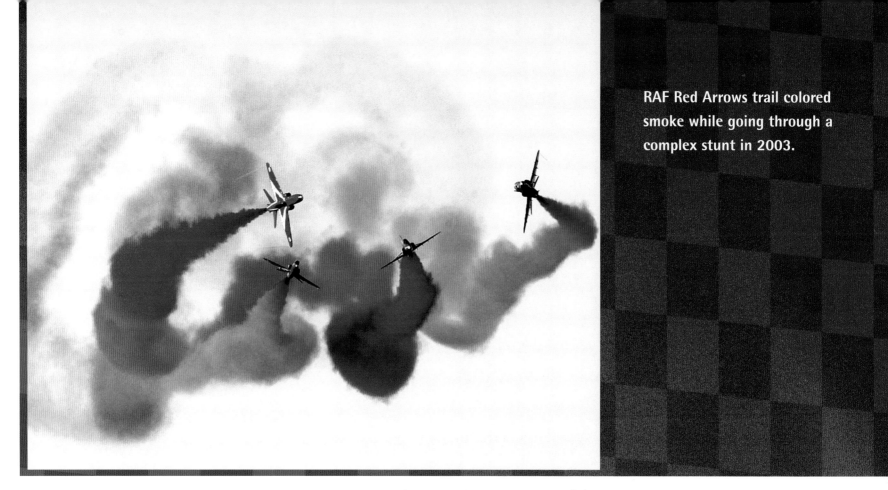

RAF Red Arrows trail colored smoke while going through a complex stunt in 2003.

Section High Alpha

The slowest move the Blue Angels perform is the section high alpha. Two jets slow down to just 144 miles (232 km) per hour and climb side by side at a 45-degree angle. After maneuvers at much higher speeds, the planes almost look as if they're standing still.

Formations are just one part of the demo, though. Pilots thrill the crowd with all sorts of daring moves. They roll their planes by twisting upside down and then back right side up. They release bright trails of smoke as they do big, arcing loops. They do high-speed breakaways and climbs, pointing the noses of their planes almost straight up. They fly inversions, cruising along upside down.

Dealing with G-Forces

Have you ever ridden a roller coaster? If so, you know that you feel lighter when you're going downhill and heavier when you're in a sharp turn. These are g-forces at work. G-forces are a lot stronger in an air show jet. As pilots speed up and turn, the g-forces cause their bodies to feel as if they are as much as seven times heavier than they really are. Most pilots wear special flight suits to help them deal with this problem. The suits squeeze their legs to force blood to the head. Because the suits are constantly adjusting, they could cause a pilot's hands to move slightly. But even the slightest movements can be disastrous when planes are only a couple of feet apart. So some air show jet pilots can't wear these suits. Instead, they condition their bodies to the g-forces. They also learn special breathing techniques that help force blood to the brain.

In one popular stunt, an inverted plane flies so close to the top of a right-side-up plane that their canopies (clear covers over the pilots' cockpits) are almost touching.

Many teams also have solo pilots. They do stunts at extreme speeds. The high-speed pass always gets a crowd going. To do a pass, two planes fly straight at each other, just missing a crash. The planes may both roll as they pass. This exciting move gets a lot of "oohs" and "ahhs" from below.

Two Thunderbirds perform a high-speed pass in their F-16 Fighting Falcons.

When a demo is done—usually after about 40 minutes—the pilots land the planes. Fans of all ages get in line for the chance to meet the brave pilots. The pilots are happy to talk about the demo and answer questions. They pose for pictures and sign autographs. Interacting with the fans is a big part of the job. Often the fans also get a chance to see the planes close-up. They can run their hands along the smooth outside of the plane. They can smell the fumes of the jet fuel and look inside the cockpit. It's a great way to get a real firsthand experience of the exciting world of air show jets.

Top: Major Rob Skelton high fives an air show fan during the Thunderbirds' first trip to Ireland in 2007. *Bottom:* Blue Angels pilots sign autographs after a flight demonstration in Louisiana in 2008.

A-4 Skyhawk

The Skyhawk—characterized by its delta (triangle-shaped) wings—was one of the navy's best attack aircraft in the late 1950s and early 1960s. By 1974 the Blue Angels wanted a smaller, more maneuverable airplane, and the Skyhawk fit the bill. The team used it until 1985, when it switched to the F/A-18 Hornet.

Specifications

Length: 40 feet 3 inches (12.2 m)

Wingspan: 26 feet 6 inches (8.4 m)

Engine: Pratt & Whitney J52-P8A turbojet

Thrust: 9,300 pounds (4,218 kg)

Top Speed: 673 miles (1,083 km) per hour

BAE Hawk

The Hawk, which made its first flight in 1974, is the jet of the RAF Red Arrows. The small plane replaced the Gnat in 1979. It's also the jet of the Finnish Air Force's Midnight Hawks. It is used mainly as a training jet but can also serve as a small combat aircraft.

Specifications

Length: 39 feet (12 m)

Wingspan: 30 feet 10 inches (9.4 m)

Engine: Rolls-Royce Adour Mk 151

Thrust: 5,200 pounds (2,359 kg)

Top Speed: 645 miles (1,037 km) per hour

U.S. Navy Blue Angels, A–4F Skyhawk

RAF Red Arrows, BAE Hawks

CT-114 Tutor

The Tutor is the only airplane the Snowbirds have ever flown. These training jets were designed and built in Canada, a source of pride to team members and members of the Canadian Forces. The white-and-red paint scheme represents the colors of Canada's flag.

Specifications

Length: 32 feet (9.8 m)

Wingspan: 36 feet 6 inches (11 m)

Engine: General Electric J85-CAN-40 axial flow turbojet

Thrust: 2,700 pounds (1,225 kg)

Top Speed: 470 miles (757 km) per hour

F-4 Phantom II

The F-4 Phantom II is the only jet that both the Blue Angels and the Thunderbirds flew. Unfortunately, it didn't last long with either team. The F-4 was big and bulky. Its twin engines burned a lot of fuel and were costly to maintain. Both teams stopped using the F-4 in 1974.

Specifications

Length: 63 feet (19 m)

Wingspan: 38 feet 7 inches (12 m)

Engine: two General Electric J79-GE-17A turbojets

Thrust: 35,800 pounds (16,240 kg)

Top Speed: 1,485 miles (2,390 km) per hour

Canadian Snowbirds,
CT–114 Tutors

U.S. Navy Blue Angels, F–4 Phantom II

F6F-5 Hellcat

The original airplane of the Blue Angels wasn't
even a jet. The F6F-5 Hellcat, a propeller-driven
plane, had been a carrier-based fighter in World
War II. Roy "Butch" Voris picked the Hellcat as the
Blue Angels' plane for its speed and easy handling.
The plane was replaced after just a few months.

Specifications
Length: 33 feet 7 inches (10 m)
Wingspan: 42 feet 10 inches (13 m)
Engine: Pratt & Whitney R-2800-10W
     two-row radial engine
Horsepower: 2,000 (1,491 kilowatts)
Top Speed: 380 miles (610 km) per hour

F9F-2 Panther

For the Blue Angels, the jet era began in 1949
with the F9F-2 Panther. The Panther—the most
heavily used jet of the Korean War—was a huge
step up in speed and power. Two years later, the
team switched to the upgraded F9F-5 Panther.

Specifications
Length: 37 feet 5 inches (11.3 m)
Wingspan: 38 feet (11.6 m)
Engine: Pratt & Whitney J42-P-6/P-8 turbojet
Thrust: 5,950 pounds (2,699 kg)
Top Speed: 575 miles (925 km) per hour

U.S. Navy, F6F Hellcat

U.S. Navy Blue Angels, F9F-2 Panther

F-16C/D Fighting Falcon

The U.S. Air Force classifies the Fighting Falcon as a compact, multirole fighter. It's built to go fast and handle well, making it a perfect air show jet. The Thunderbirds started flying the F-16A in 1982 and adopted the updated F-16C/D 10 years later. The airplane's record with the team and in the field makes it one of the most successful fighters in air force history.

Specifications
Length: 49 feet 5 inches (15 m)
Wingspan: 32 feet 8 inches (10 m)
Engine: Pratt & Whitney F100-PW-200/220/229
　　　or General Electric F110-GE-100/129
Thrust: 27,000 pounds (12,250 kg)
Top Speed: 1,500 miles (2,415 km) per hour

F-84F Thunderstreak

The U.S. Air Force Thunderbirds flew this swept-wing jet from 1955 to 1956. The F-84F was supposed to be an improvement on the F-84 Thunderjet, but it suffered from performance problems. The Thunderbirds replaced it with the superior F-100 Super Sabre in 1956.

Specifications
Length: 43 feet 5 inches (13.2 m)
Wingspan: 33 feet 7 inches (10.3 m)
Engine: Wright J-65-W-3 turbojet
Thrust: 7,220 pounds (3,275 kg)
Top Speed: 695 miles (1,119 km) per hour

U.S. Air Force
Thunderbirds, F–16C/D

U.S. Air Force Thunderbirds,
F–84F Thunderstreak

F-100 Super Sabre

The U.S. Air Force's first supersonic jet was the airplane that really put the Thunderbirds on the map. This big fighter bomber entered air force service in 1954. The team flew the Super Sabre from 1956 to 1969. Its speed and handling made it a useful plane into the early 1970s. The Thunderbirds flew the third model of the Super Sabre, the F-100C.

Specifications
Length: 53 feet 11 inches (16 m)
Wingspan: 38 feet 10 inches (12 m)
Engine: Pratt & Whitney J57-P-21
Thrust: 16,000 pounds (7,260 kg)
Top Speed: 900 miles (1,450 km) per hour

F/A-18 Hornet

The Blue Angels have flown the F/A-18 Hornet since 1986. The Hornet first entered U.S. Navy service in 1983. In the field, this powerful strike fighter often takes off from and lands on aircraft carriers. Although a newer version of the airplane, the F/A-18 E/F Super Hornet, has become the navy's main strike fighter, the Hornet remains the plane of choice for the Blue Angels.

Specifications
Length: 56 feet (17 m)
Wingspan: 40 feet 5 inches (12 m)
Engine: two General Electric F404-GE-400
low-bypass, turbofan engines
Thrust: About 32,000 pounds (14,515 kg)
Top Speed: About 1,200 miles (1,932 km) per hour

U.S. Air Force Thunderbirds, F–100 Super Sabre

U.S. Navy Blue Angels, F/A–18 Hornet
(shown flying upside down)

Folland Gnat

The Folland Gnat, a small British trainer jet, was the original airplane of the RAF Red Arrows. The Red Arrows got the planes from a previous air show team, the RAF Yellowjackets. The small Gnat was easy to maneuver and cheap to maintain—a perfect combination. The Red Arrows used it until 1979, when the BAE Hawk replaced it.

Specifications
Length: 28 feet 8 inches (8.7 m)
Wingspan: 22 feet 1 inch (6.7 m)
Engine: Bristol-Siddeley Orpheus 701-01 turbojet
Thrust: 4,705 pounds (2,134 kg)
Top Speed: 695 miles (1,120 km) per hour

L-39C Albatross

The L-39C Albatross is a trainer jet that the former Soviet Union used in the late 1960s and 1970s. In recent decades, many of these jets have been sold to private citizens, mostly because they're cheap compared to most jets. Vyazma Rus, a Russian formation team, has flown the Albatross since 1987. The Patriots, another private demo team, has flown the Albatross since 1999.

Specifications
Length: 41 feet (13 m)
Wingspan: 31 feet (9.4 m)
Engine: AI-25TL
Thrust: 3,800 pounds (1,725 kg)
Top Speed: 560 miles (900 km) per hour

RAF Red Arrows, Folland Gnat

Vyazma Rus, L-39C Albatross

Glossary

aerial: a move done in the air

barnstormer: a pilot who traveled around the country in the 1920s, putting on air shows for small towns and cities

bomber: a plane designed to drop bombs on enemy targets

dogfight: a battle between two airplanes in the air

fighter: a plane designed to shoot down enemy planes and other targets

formation: an arrangement of airplanes flying together

inversion: a move in which a plane flies upside down

newbie: a new, or training, member of a demo team

precision: being very accurate or exact

propeller: the set of rapidly spinning blades on the front of an aircraft that pulls a plane through the air. Jet technology has largely replaced the propeller on airplanes.

subsonic: unable to travel as fast as the speed of sound

supersonic: able to travel faster than the speed of sound

thrust: the forward force produced by a jet engine

trainer: a plane used to teach pilots how to fly

wingman: a pilot who flies behind and to the side of a lead plane, off of one of the leader's wings

Selected Bibliography

Dempsey, Daniel V. *A Tradition of Excellence: Canada's Air Show Team Heritage*. Victoria, BC: High Flight Enterprises, 2002.

Hurley, Graham. *Air Show: A Year in the Life of the World's Largest Military Air Show*. London: Orion, 1998.

Thunderbirds Alumni Association. *We Rode the Thunder: The Autobiography of the United States Air Force Thunderbirds; Celebrating Our Golden Anniversary*. Evansville, IN: M. T. Pub., 2003.

Veronico, Nicholas A., and Marga B. Fritze. *Blue Angels: 50 Years of Precision Flight*. Osceola, WI: Motorbooks International, 1996.

Further Reading

Dartford, Mark. *Fighter Planes*. Minneapolis: Lerner Publications Company, 2004.

Donovan, Sandy. *The U.S. Air Force*. Minneapolis: Lerner Publications Company, 2005.

Gaffney, Timothy R. *Air Show Pilots and Airplanes*. Berkeley Heights, NJ: Enslow, 2001.

Websites

Blue Angels: Official Website
http://www.blueangels.navy.mil
The home page of the Blue Angels includes news, pictures, and video of the team's planes, pilots, and other officers, as well as the team's full schedule.

Canadian Air Force Snowbirds
http://www.snowbirds.forces.gc.ca
This page tells you all you need to know about the Snowbirds. It has a detailed history of the team, a section on all of its different formations, and lots of photos.

RAF Red Arrows
http://www.raf.mod.uk/reds
Check out this site for all the latest information on the Red Arrows, including a fans' area and a detailed behind-the-scenes look at the team.

Thunderbirds: Offical Website
http://thunderbirds.airforce.com
See pictures and video of the Thunderbirds at their home page. The site includes news, a schedule, and detailed information about the team's officers and planes.

Index

About the Author

Matt Doeden is a freelance author and editor living in Minnesota. He has written and edited hundreds of books for both children and adults, including several others in the Motor Mania series.

About the Consultants

Richard Bihler is a pilot and airplane enthusiast. He lives in Prior Lake, MN.

Justin D. Pyle is a technical sergeant in the U.S. Air Force. He has served as an aerial photojournalist (1997–2000) and art director (2005–2008) with the U.S. Air Force Air Demonstration Squadron, Thunderbirds.

Photo Acknowledgments

The images in this book are used with the permission of: U.S. Navy Photo by Mass Communication Specialist Seaman Omar A. Dominquez, p. 5; National Archives, p. 6 (W&C 0590); © Popperfoto/Getty Images, p. 6 (bottom left); © Bettmann/CORBIS, p. 7; © Hulton Archive/Getty Images, p. 8; © Firstblueangel.com, pp. 9 (both), 17, 38 (bottom); AP Photo/Str, pp. 10, 43 (top); © Laura Westlund/Independent Picture Service, pp. 11, 30; © age fotostock/SuperStock, pp. 13, 37 (top); U.S. Air Force photo by Chad Bellay, p. 14; Justin D. Pyle, pp. 15, 16, 25 (top), 29, 33 (top); © Scott Olson/Getty Images, pp. 18-19; U.S. Navy Photo by Mass Communication Specialist 2nd Class Lynn Friant, p. 20; U.S. Navy Photo by Mass Communication Specialist 2nd Class Christopher Brown, p. 21; © Saul Loeb/AFP/Getty Images, p. 22; U.S. Air Force photo/Larry McTighe, p. 23; © Nader Khouri/Contra Costa Times/ZUMA Press, p. 24; U.S. Navy Photo by Photographer's Mate 2nd Class Johansen Laurel, p. 25 (bottom); U.S. Navy Photo, pp. 26, 28, 43 (bottom); AP Photo/Daytona Beach News-Journal, Nigel Cook, p. 27 (left); U.S. Navy Photo by Photographer's Mate 1st Class Casey Akins, p. 27 (right); © Mohammed Mahjoub/AFP/Getty Images, p. 31; AP Photo/Paul Warner, p. 32; U.S. Navy Photo by Mass Communication Specialist 1st Class Kimberly R. Stephens, p. 33 (bottom); PH2 Paul O'Mara/United States Department of Defense, p. 34 (top); © Hideo Kurihara/Alamy, p. 34 (bottom); United States Department of Defense, p. 35 (top); © Joe Fox/Alamy, p. 35 (bottom); © Bill Bachmann/Alamy, p. 36 (top); © Ron Rentfrow, pp. 36 (bottom), 37 (bottom); © Thierry GRUN - Aero/Alamy, p. 38 (top); © SuperStock, Inc./SuperStock, p. 39 (top); © J.R. Eyerman/Time & Life Pictures/Getty Images, p. 39 (bottom); U.S. Air Force photo/Airman 1st Class Chad M. Kellum, p. 40 (top); © LeighSmithImages/Alamy, p. 40 (bottom); U.S. Air Force photo/Master Sgt. Jack Braden, p. 41 (top); U.S. Air Force photo, pp. 41 (bottom), 42 (top); U.S. Navy Photo by Photographer's Mate 2nd Class Daniel J. McLain, p. 42 (bottom); © Malcolm Fife/Alamy, p. 44 (top); © BG Motorsports/Alamy, p. 44 (bottom); © John Henshall/Alamy, p. 45 (top); © Yuri Kadobnov/AFP/Getty Images, p. 45 (bottom).

Front Cover: U.S. Air Force photo/David Armer.